Forgiveness
and beyond

Stefka Harp

Forgiveness and beyond
© Stefka Mladenova 2015

All rights reserved. No part of this publication may be reproduced, stored in a retrieval system, or transmitted in any form or by any means, electronic, mechanical, photocopying, recording or otherwise, without the prior written permission of the author.

National Library of Australia Cataloguing-in-Publication entry
Creator: Harp, Stefka, author.
Title: Forgiveness & beyond/Stafka Harp
ISBN: 9780992304065 (paperback)
Subjects: Australian poetry — 21st century
           Forgiveness — Poetry
Dewey number: A821.4

Published with the assistance of www.wordwrightediting.com.au

Images courtesy of clker.com.

www.stefkaharp.com

Forgiveness and beyond

Contents

Acknowledgements v

Introduction vi

Dedication vii

Forgive yourself 1

Asking for forgiveness 2

Forgiveness brings healing 4

Always forgive 6

Reward yourself 7

Rejoice in forgiving 8

Forgive and let go 10

The power of forgiveness 12

Do not provoke jealousy 14

Delight in praying 16

Set yourself free 18

Mud sticks, so they say 20

Your thoughts 22

Patience 23

Joy and cheers 24

Competence 25

Own your feelings 26

Inner strength 28

Confidence 29

Rejoice in the truth ... 30

Doom and gloom ... 32

Excitement ... 33

Choose to be happy ... 34

Be in harmony ... 36

Joy upon me ... 37

The power of the mind ... 38

Angels and saints ... 40

I am who I am ... 41

My eternal friend ... 42

Resist envy ... 43

I give unconditional love ... 44

Jealousy ... 46

Karma ... 47

About the author ... 48

Forgiveness and beyond

Acknowledgements

I wish to express my deep and sincere gratitude to my parents for teaching me the value of life — how to love and be happy as well as show kindness; and to my siblings, for being a part of my life.

My thanks, too, to the Australian Government for opening the door for me to migrate and become a permanent resident; to experience a different kind of life, culture and customs, which has been very enriching, enlightening and eye-opening. I am very grateful for the opportunity I have been given and guided to get to the point I am at.

Sincere gratitude to:

- my daughter for her patience and loving assistance in proofreading my work
- Alison Leader for her editing
- my publishing advisor for assistance given
- my niece Maria and my loyal friends who were willing to read my manuscripts and give constructive comments and feedback.

Stefka Harp

Introduction

This publication is not only to do with forgiveness, but incorporates a lot more, including negative feelings such as envy, jealousy, slander and the like.

The negative feelings and thoughts released propagate, and there is an ongoing perpetuation in life about which we wonder.

To change our thinking, we have to become aware of our thoughts and start to break the habit of negative thinking — turning it into love and loving thoughts instead. Forgiveness is a part of this process.

Happy reading

Stefka Harp

Forgiveness and beyond

Dedication

Everything I write and have written so far is dedicated to my family and the divine within, which has guided me through life. At times my ignorance and oblivion to the facts revealed has led to strife and suffering. But these experiences have given me the much-needed fuel for my writings, and I hope they will help others. Life is like a jigsaw puzzle. Some things are meant to happen so that the pieces fit within that puzzle.

S.H.

Forgiveness and beyond

Failing to forgive yourself and so,
Opportunity missed to spiritually grow,
Receive blessings from the divine,
Glory would come in good time.
Inspire loving thoughts and persist,
Visualise serenity you would kiss,
Enjoyment should be on your list.

Yes my friend, it is a breeze,
Only if you don't freeze.
Urgently embrace all those loving thoughts,
Ready to turn them into loving words.
Seize the moment and bless the world, for
Ever more forgive yourself and behold,
Love everlasting in delight,
Farewell guilt and shame overnight.

Stefka Harp

Ask for forgiveness if you dare,
Surely it makes it easier through a prayer,
Keen as one would, send out loving thoughts,
Instantly they become powerful words.
Nullify the wrong deeds, leaving them behind,
Gracefully receive blessing from the Divine.

Fair to say, one is halfway there,
Obscure it might appear,
Remember, it's darkest before the night
                                    disappears.

Forgiveness and beyond

Forgiveness is a habit and to dwell on,
Over joy in forgiving as well,
Reassure self, this is the way to go,
Grasp the wisdom of forgiveness forever more.
Impress it on your mind,
Validate your need and trust the Divine,
Endlessly that makes one come alive,
Necessary to show love and be kind,
Enforcing the mind to continue the same way,
Sure enough serenity will come some day,
Signalling the habit of forgiveness,
                here to stay.

Feed your mind with loving thoughts,
Onset to spark loving words,
Raise your consciousness without a fuss,
Gladness in one's soul is a plus.
Instantly will go and align,
Vigorously with the Divine,
Eliminating what's not desired,
Never to turn back and acquire,
Elements of negative desire.
Smile with a humble gratitude,
Sustenance of one's attitude.

Beyond all questions in your mind,
Request forgiveness and be kind,
Increase one's awareness and do not blame,
Nifty way to release the pain.
Grant yourself to be happy with delight,
Sense the change in your health overnight.

Forgiveness and beyond

Hold dear and persevere,
Endless blessings without fear,
Allow for the soul to blossom and cheer,
Love will be both dear and sincere,
Indulge in having good health and be gay,
Nevertheless as it may,
Grasp the wisdom of forgiving every day.

Although not possible all the time,
Love and hope you're sure to find,
Wisdom in the forgiveness and prayer,
Amazingly, self-talk will get you there.
Yes my dears, away with fears,
Simple forgiveness will shift gears.

Forgiveness is for your peace of mind,
Occasion to celebrate and know the Divine,
Readiness for ice to melt down,
Gently if you must, but do not fool around.
Imagine your forgiving soul has been crowned,
Visualise divine light and do not worry,
Earnest well-wishing to all is a glory.

Forgiveness and beyond

Refresh your memory and be fair,
Each time you wanted to declare,
Well and truly reward is due,
Always dismissed it as not in view,
Restore faith in you and the Divine,
Desire to reward yourself just for being alive.

Yes, go ahead with full steam,
Once in a while live the dream,
Urgently give yourself a pat on the shoulder,
Remarkably, it will do a wonder,
Stand high and feel grand,
Eager loving thoughts to send,
Love and forgiveness as well,
Farewell doubt and fear, and no need to dwell.

Stefka Harp

Redemption is due,
Eagerness to forgive is the clue.
Judge not, whatever you do,
Only forgiveness should be in view.
Innermost peace and serenity,
Certainly will bring back sanity,
Endless happiness instead of suffering.

In God we trust,
Never doubt nor let it rust.

Forgiveness and beyond

Forgiveness is a wonderful deed,
One that would set you free,
Reason to celebrate you would agree,
Great life is for you to declare,
Integrate loving thoughts and prayer,
Vow to be kind if you dare.
Infinitely be sincere,
None other but the Divine,
Graciously will shine in time.

Stefka Harp

Forgive first and foremost,
Overjoy in doing so without getting lost.
Remember it will set you free,
Glory in letting go to a degree.
Impart on the count of nine,
Vigorously impress it on your mind,
End the pain by being kind.

Allow, if you must, yourself to cry,
Necessary for love to thrive,
Delight in being alive.

Forgiveness and beyond

Love does not blame,
Eases the pain by the same,
Thus let go and aim to attain,

Graceful love forever to stay,
Oneness to restore and be gay.

Take a challenge and declare,
Hence you are going to have a prayer,
Energising yourself to prepare.

Pride must be swallowed fast,
Otherwise the prayer will only stir dust,
Weary one may become and give up.
Envisage success and take it to heart,
Remember to say thanks with delight.

Obedience to oneself and the Divine, with
Faith and hope as the Holy Grail.

Forgiveness and beyond

Falter not, no doubt,
Odd may it seem, it strengthens self-esteem,
Raise one's hat and show respect,
Graceful forgiveness one will detect.
Indeed, feelings of guilt to redirect,
Veer into having loving thoughts instead,
Enough for yourself and the rest,
Namely everything on the planet to be blessed.
Enjoy sending forgiving thoughts with a smile,
Seek forgiveness from others and the Divine,
Say a prayer and forgive, leaving past behind.

Stefka Harp

Do the hokey-pokey all around,
Occasion to be on the lookout,

Never provoke jealousy in vain,
Overall just to spite and enrage,
Thus sending someone insane.

Penalty for it could be high,
Rest assured you might have to hide.
Otherwise trust others like yourself
Very best way to show them how,
Openly giving the benefit of the doubt.
Kick the habit of jealous provocation,
Earn trust, tell the truth with veneration.

Forgiveness and beyond

Joking does not make it better,
Escape the trap and leave the joke for later,
Address the issue with love and care,
Lesson to be learned and be aware,
Occasion to rejoice and dwell,
Unworthy provocation farewell,
Something to celebrate and ensure,
Yielding love and joy all the more.

Stefka Harp

Designate time for prayer,
Elate the spirit by chanting with care.
Let the wisdom within guide,
It is important not to show pride.
Gently send your loving prayer,
Heavenly father will declare
Trust in its integrity and be fair.

If you waste your time at all,
Namely on love and prayer,

Forgiveness and beyond

Persevere and be precise,
Reassure self this is the way to go in delight,
At long last one will see the light,
Yank the harshness with all your might.
Innermost soul will do the rest,
Necessary to cancel undesirables at best,
Grant yourself to feel blessed.

Seek forgiveness no matter what,
Ever more so day and night,
Tender loving thoughts in delight.

Yearn to be a free spirit,
Obey the Divine within,
Unify and take a bow,
Romance the idea to vow,
Serenity to come upon,
Electrifying spirit to make you thrilled,
Life abundant over spilled,
Freedom to flow for the mind to spin.

Forgiveness and beyond

Forgive everyone and everything around,
Regardless if there's a reason or not,
Enjoy forgiving without doubt,
Empower with loving thoughts as a habit.

Stefka Harp

Mud sticks, might as well be, but,
Unlikely to all around,
Depending on the divine crown.

Slandering is a slaughter,
The beauty of it all,
It makes you stronger,
Continuously reflecting divine light,
Keen to guide in delight,
Scarcely affected in the slight.

Sooner or later the deeds will bounce,
Only to come back and pronounce,

Forgiveness and beyond

The slander sent out,
Hence is coming back no doubt,
Ever-so-strong to hunt the slanderer down,
Yes, the sent-out energy will be around.

Seems, mud only sticks to mud,
An angel shines near and far,
Yes it's true, regardless of being soiled,
      smudged or dipped in tar.

Stefka Harp

You can think what you like,
Out goes projection overnight,
Unduly but truly,
Reflection will come surely.

Thence self-esteem to boost
Home your thoughts would come to roost.
Oppose if something so bizarre,
Ultimately change to what you desire.
Gain confidence and admire,
Hopefully you would inspire,
Tremendous attention to acquire,
Selective thought to transpire.

Forgiveness and beyond

Pretend you are in a play,
Allowing you to be gay,
Then continue with the game,
Imagine patience all the way.
Empower yourself with a loving care,
No way could you fail,
Competence will start to flair,
Eliminating the scare.

Join in and be brave,
  Over and above play it safe,
  Yearn for a good day and do not stray.

  Allow the divine to guide,
  Necessary for one to thrive,
  Delight in life without pride.

  Chase the dream of happiness,
  Hope brings gayness,
  Empower the mind to be thrilled,
  Expect inner peace and it will begin,
  Radiance and joy will be manifesting,
  Scintillating and divinely caressing.

Forgiveness and beyond

Cheer and chant my dear friend,
Over and above and make it grand,
Make believe in one's ability,
Patiently yet with agility.
Endure the test; it is not a guess,
Thorough enjoyment to manifest,
Enhance it with loving thoughts,
Nullify the undesired in words,
Competent thoughts and feelings in time,
Earnestly will lead you to know the Divine.

Stefka Harp

Openly and honestly,
Will yourself
Never to blame or condemn.

Yes by yearning to displace
Overflow of feelings,
Ugly or otherwise,
Rejoice instead, and own them all.

Forgiveness and beyond

First and foremost forgive,
Even when you don't feel,
Ever so powerful enough to do so,
Loving attitude confidence will restore,
Inevitable to acknowledge and make sure, to
Notice the feelings yet again,
Grant yourself peace to feel the positive gain,
Sense the pleasure by releasing the pain.

Indulge in thinking you are strong,
Never for a moment get it wrong,
Never turn the sting on yourself.
Ensure to give, love and care,
Rather urgently, well deserved.

Sow the seeds of faith and grow,
Tomorrow will be time to plough.
Raise the value of self and know,
Eminently it is to believe so.
None other but the Divine,
Gently will find,
To give the strength you adore,
Hope and faith galore.

Forgiveness and beyond

Create a loving attitude,
Openly and honestly,
Neither doubt nor falter.
Face your fears and fear no more,
Integrate tender loving care,
Delight in who you are,
Embrace it with all your might,
Note the changes in your heart,
Confidence is sure to flow,
Encouragement to get you through the door.

Stefka Harp

Ratify in your mind what you need,
Express feelings with glee,
Journey through life eagerly and be brave,
On the lookout as you may.
Inspire love and truth in your heart,
Caress loving thoughts in delight,
Establish a habit day and night.

Integrate tender loving care,
Necessary to say your prayer,

Forgiveness and beyond

Trust the Divine within,
Hesitate and you will be quitting,
Emerge victorious and smile in greeting.

Thrill when truth is told,
Roar, it is a pot of gold,
Unreal might seem so,
Treasure it just the same and uphold,
Heavens above will bring joy to the world.

Dawn is here, sun is rising,
Open the door to greet the buzzing,
Offering a pleasant day,
Moment to cherish and be gay.

Anticipate the day with rapture,
Necessary brilliant light to capture,
Divine happiness to find and nurture.

Gloominess will dissipate on the go,
Long before you know,
Opportunity to explore forever more.
Off it goes, happiness to restore,
Merriment is sure forever to flow.

Forgiveness and beyond

Emerge from the shadows of the doubt,
X, Y, Z, it is not about,
Clarify your desires,
Indulge in believing and admire,
Time to say thanks and praise the Lord,
Ensuring happiness galore,
Majestically will lift your soul,
Excitement will fill your heart,
Notably some progress overnight,
Time after time, day and night.

Stefka Harp

Conceive happiness in one's mind, the
Higher will take you over the line,
Onset for a change though,
On and on forever more,
Smile, instead of a frown,
Ensure always to love and grow.

Time and again,
Or as often as one can.

Forgiveness and beyond

Be on the lookout,
Eagerly without a doubt,

Happiness will show a sign,
Amazingly to those who are kind,
Persevere and endure,
Praise self and endear,
Yes, happiness is here.

Stefka Harp

Be the change you would like to see,
Express your views with glee.

Inspire excellence and declare,
Never to judge nor condemn.

Hence forward marching by,
Attuned to the well wishes of the day,
Reclaim the Divine within,
Merriment for sure to get in,
One's pride being swallowed,
No one will ever know, and
Yet, harmony continuously will flow.

Forgiveness and beyond

Just to say hi,
   Opportunity to be kind,
   Yearning for peace in my mind,

Utmost sincerity forever more,
Possibility to learn and spiritually grow,
Only way to live a life,
Never doubt nor deny.

Memories always there forever so,
Emotions as well, only pain forever gone.

Stefka Harp

The mind is like a child,
Harmless and possibly kind,
End result is, it does not mind,

Precisely what's real and what's not,
Over and above it only knows,
What you tell it and it's so,
Endlessly forever more,
Right or wrong it follows on.

Open to the universe and above all,
Follow your heart and truth be told.

Forgiveness and beyond

The impression on your mind,
Hard and fast would come to shine,
Ever more so, thank the Divine.

Mend the wrongs and do not miss,
Inner most peace you would kiss,
Never quit hoping, to
Discover the power within.

Stefka Harp

Angels here, saints there,
Nowhere and everywhere,
Gracefully praising and praying,
Endless blessings to come our way,
Love, peace and harmony without saying,
Saturation of the above here to stay.

Always on the go and forever gay,
Never rest but pray,
Doing what they love is their play.

Seems to be the game of the day,
Another enjoyable one on the way,
Immense pleasure to explore,
Never a chore or a bore,
Tremendous excitement galore,
Saints and angels our loving core.

Forgiveness and beyond

I have a loving attitude on the go,

Always perfecting and moving along,
Memories to cherish and be strong.

Who I am I hope to be respected for,
Hence, along the way accepted so,
Oneness to be resurrected and glow,

If others want me to be somebody else,

An instant awareness will be prancing,
Manifesting who I am with joyful dancing.

Stefka Harp

Many moons had past,
Yet, here we are at last.

Everlasting soul always knows,
The way one's life goes,
Ending is a new beginning.
Rejoice and celebrate in the knowing,
Now and forever love regenerates,
Allowing us to uphold dignity and be kind,
Leap for joy and send love divine.

Friends we have been forever,
Reunited many times over,
Indeed every new life is a pleasure,
Event always to treasure.
Never doubt nor ponder,
Destiny is certainly a wonder.

Forgiveness and beyond

Restless divine child you are,
Everyone else is afar,
Something is gnawing at you,
Inkling to catch up and compare,
Seize the moment and become aware,
Trust your loving soul and declare.

Envy is something to farewell,
Never to come across again.
Vivaciously ask love to come by,
You don't have to ask why.

Stefka Harp

Inside of me there is a child,

   Generous and kind,
   Inkling to inspire,
   Vigorous and loving thoughts to transpire, to
   Embrace the love I desire.

   Universal love is powerful and strong,
   Nurture it I do, for as long,
   Continually without a fuss,
   Oneness with the divine is a plus. I
   Nourish my soul with a loving thought,
   Delighted to give love to the world,
   Indefinite, expecting nothing in return,
   Timeless gift in my life to attain.
   Infinitely if I can, without a blame,
   Onward marching by, on course to stay,
   Noble soul showing the way,
   At long last to shine and be holy,
   Life, full of love and laughter to make me jolly.

Forgiveness and beyond

Love is powerful when given away,
Openly and unconditionally as I may,
Vigorously with all my heart,
Elevating my soul and others' in delight.

Journey your life and show love,
Embrace life with all your heart,
Always, no matter what.
Learn to love even if it does not feel right,
Own the feelings; it's not going to bite,
Unload the burden of jealousy with delight.
Surrender to love instead; have a good night,
Y? Where love is, everything turns out alright.

Forgiveness and beyond

Karma is, one gets what one gives out,
Always ten times or more in strength,
Radiance and glory or tears might be pouring,
Merriment will come with loving thoughts,
Away with tears and in with cheers.

Stefka Harp

About the author

Stefka was born during World War II in a small village tucked away in the foothills of a big mountain in Eastern Macedonia.

Her family, like others in the village, gained their food from the land. It was a self-sufficient household. This lifestyle built much confidence in her and her siblings.

She migrated to Australia in 1972, where she still resides. She finished her degree, and a diploma in counselling, and gained jobs in the welfare sector.

The last seven years before retirement were spent in the DV sector. While working with people she noticed the power of thought in relation to destiny. She believes that when people change their thinking and implement positive and loving thoughts, life changes for better. Prayer, forgiveness, hope and faith go hand in hand with a positive attitude.

Academic achievements

Diploma of Community Services Management

    Southbank Institute of TAFE 2006

Diploma in Counselling

    Australian Institute of Counsellors 1993–1994

Bachelor of Arts Degree (Major Psychology)

    University of Queensland 1989

Economics, book keeping & accounting

    Business Studies College (Macedonia)

www.ingramcontent.com/pod-product-compliance
Lightning Source LLC
Chambersburg PA
CBHW061257040426
42444CB00010B/2401